MS Power Point

Davinder Singh Minhas

RISING SUN

RISING SUN
an imprint of
New Dawn Press

NEW DAWN PRESS GROUP
New Dawn Press, Inc., 244 South Randall Rd # 90, Elgin, IL 60123
e-mail: sales@newdawnpress.com
New Dawn Press, 2 Tintern Close, Slough, Berkshire, SL1-2TB, UK
e-mail: ndpuk@newdawnpress.com
        sterlingdis@yahoo.co.uk

New Dawn Press (An Imprint of Sterling Publishers (P) Ltd.)

A-59, Okhla Industrial Area, Phase-II, New Delhi-110020
e-mail: sterlingpublishers@touchtelindia.net
        Ghai@nde.vsnl.net.in

© 2005, New Dawn Press

Printed at Sterling Publishers Pvt. Ltd., New Delhi

Contents

1. Introduction — 5

2. Using AutoContent Wizard — 13

3. Creating a Blank Presentation — 17

4. Saving, Opening and Formatting a Presentation — 26

5. Adding Graphics — 32

6. Viewing and Printing Slide Show — 35

1. Introduction

Microsoft PowerPoint is a complete presentation graphics program that allows you to create professional presentations. A PowerPoint **presentation** is also known as a **slide show.** PowerPoint gives you the flexibility to make presentations using a projection device attached to a personal computer and using overhead transparencies. In addition, you can take advantage of the World Wide Web and run virtual presentations on the Internet.

PowerPoint contains several features to simplify creating a slide show. For example, you can instruct PowerPoint to create a pre-designed presentation, and then you can modify the presentation to fulfill your requirements. You can format a slide show using one of the **design templates**. You can add tables, charts, pictures, video, sound and animation effects to enhance the appearance of your presentation. You can also check the spelling or style of your slide show as you type or after you have completed designing the presentation. With the help of charts, you can make your presentation look more interesting. The two chart types are: **standard**, which includes bar, line, pie, and xy (scatter) charts; and **custom**, which displays objects such as floating bars, colored lines, and three-dimensional cones.

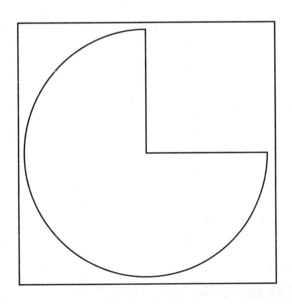

Starting and Customizing PowerPoint

To begin a new presentation in PowerPoint, the most common way is by using the **Start** button on the **Windows taskbar**. Perform the following steps to start PowerPoint and make a new presentation.

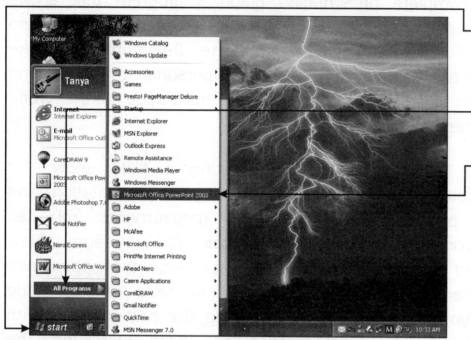

1. Click on the **start** button. The start menu will appear.

2. Click on **All Programs** in the start menu.

3. In the All Program submenu, click on **Microsoft Office PowerPoint 2003**.

The Microsoft PowerPoint window appears after a few moments.

*(In some versions of Windows, you have to click on **Programs** instead of **All Programs**.)*

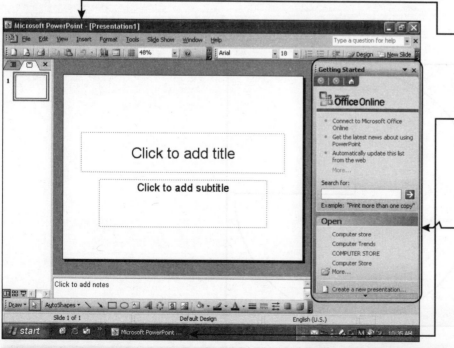

A blank presentation titled **Presentation 1** is displayed in the PowerPoint window.

The Windows taskbar displays the PowerPoint program button, indicating that PowerPoint is running.

A task pane may appear, enabling users to perform common and online tasks quickly.

After installation when you start PowerPoint for the first time, the way the window looks on the computer screen is shown in the previous page in the figure.

You will also notice a task pane displayed on the right side of the screen and the buttons on the tool bar being displayed on a single row. The task pane, which is a separate window, is used to carry out some PowerPoint tasks more efficiently and quickly.

You can close the task pane to allow maximum side space in PowerPoint window for more efficient use. The buttons on the toolbar should be displayed in two separate rows instead of sharing a single row.

Perform the following steps to close the New Workbook task pane and display the buttons of the toolbar in two separate rows.

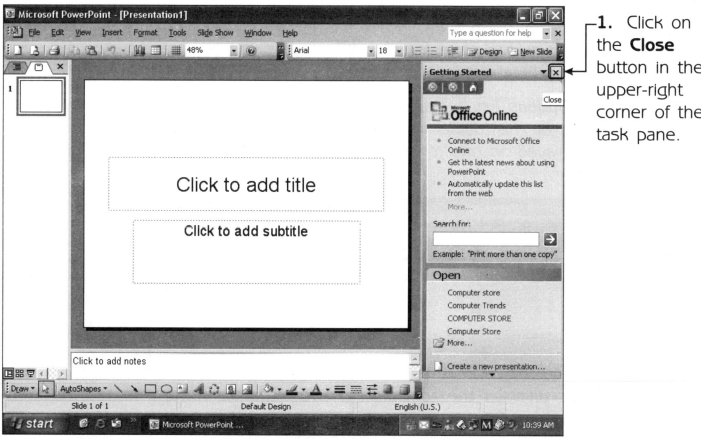

1. Click on the **Close** button in the upper-right corner of the task pane.

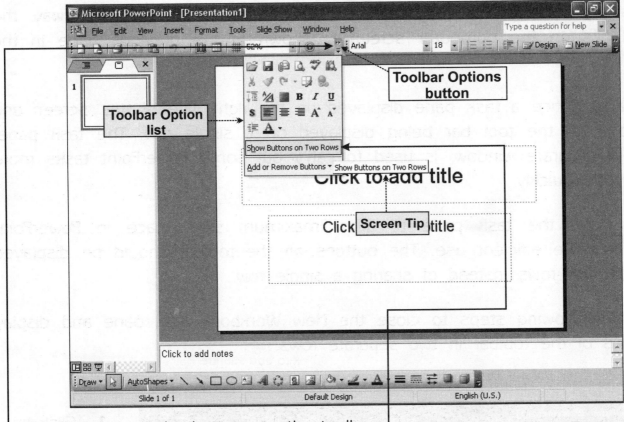

2. If you want the buttons on the toolbar to be displayed on two rows, click on the **Toolbar Options** button. A list will appear.

*The **Toolbar Options list** contains buttons that do not fit on the toolbar when the toolbar is displayed on one row.*

3. Click on **Show Buttons on Two Rows**.

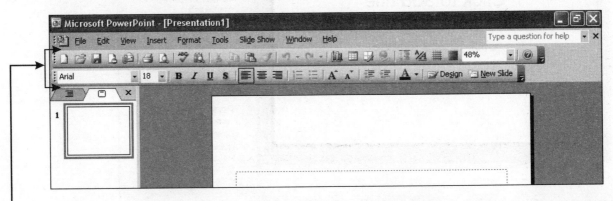

PowerPoint displays the toolbars on two separate rows. The Toolbar Options list becomes empty because all the buttons fit on the toolbar when they are displayed on two rows.

The PowerPoint Window

With the help of several items displayed in the PowerPoint window, you can perform your tasks efficiently.

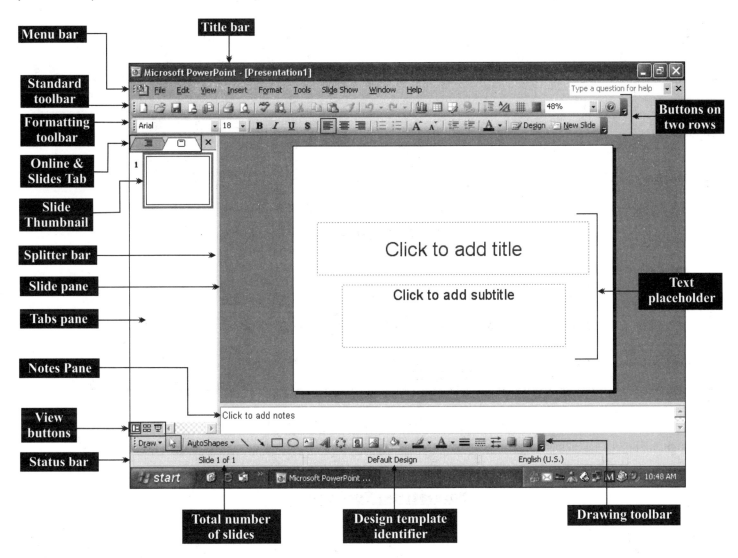

A **slide**, which contains objects such as the title, text, table, charts and drawings, is the basic unit of a PowerPoint presentation. For a PowerPoint slide, an object is the building block. The first slide is assumed to be the title slide, whose aim is to introduce the presentation to the audience. Properties or characteristics of an object are defined as **Attributes**. For instance, if you underline the title of a slide, the title is the object and the underline is the attribute. The default **slide layout** is **landscape orientation** when you start PowerPoint, where the slide width is greater than its height.

Standard, Formatting and Drawing Toolbars:
To perform frequent tasks more quickly and efficiently than the menu bar, the Standard toolbar, Formatting toolbar and Drawing toolbar are used.

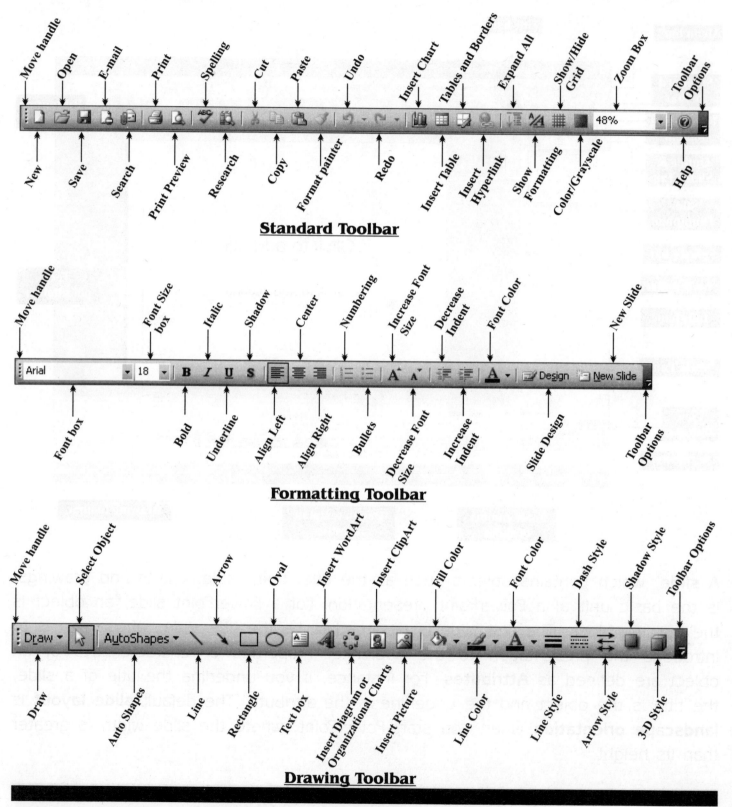

Standard Toolbar

Formatting Toolbar

Drawing Toolbar

Types of PowerPoint Views

PowerPoint offers three types of views viz, **Normal View**, **Slide Sorter View** or **Slide Show View**.

Normal View

It displays three panes: the **Tabs pane** with either the Outline tab or the Slides tab, the **Slide pane** and the **Notes pane**.

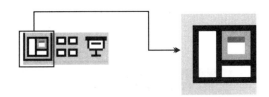

Slide Sorter View

It displays thumbnail versions of all slides in a presentation. You can then copy, cut, paste or otherwise change the slide position to modify the presentation. Slide sorter view is also used to add timings to the slide, to select animated transitions and to preview animations.

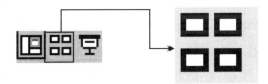

Slide Show View

This view displays the slides as an electronic presentation on the screen of your computer's monitor. Looking much like a slide projector display, you can see the effect of transitions, build effects, slide timings and animations.

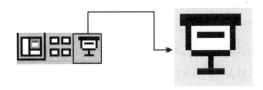

Status Bar: It is placed at the bottom of the screen above the Windows taskbar. A message area and a presentation design template identifier are present in the Status bar. The current slide number and the total number of slides in the slide show are displayed in the message area. For example, figure below the message area displays **Slide 1 of 1**. 'Slide 1' is the current slide being displayed and 'of 1' indicates that slide show contains only 1 slide. The template identifier displays Default Design, which is the template that PowerPoint uses initially.

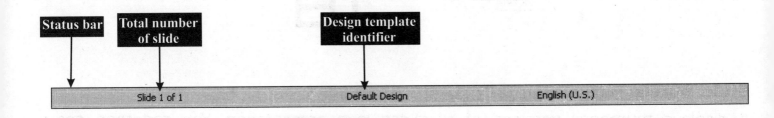

Menu Bar: A list of commands is called a menu. The menu bar is a special toolbar which includes the menu names of certain commands that you can use to retrieve, store, print and manipulate data on the presentation. When you point to a menu name on the menu bar it changes to a button. To display a name, for example, the Edit menu, click on Edit on the menu bar. A submenu is displayed if you point to a command on the menu with an arrow to its right from which you can choose a command.

A **short menu** displays the list of the most recently used commands when you click on a menu bar. The **full menu** is displayed if you wait a few seconds or once you click the arrows at the bottom of the short menu. The full menu lists all the commands associated with a menu. A full menu can also be displayed immediately by double-clicking on the menu name on the menu bar. When you display a menu, always display the full menu.

2. Using AutoContent Wizard

One can create a presentation using the **AutoContent Wizard**. The wizard asks you a series of questions and then sets up a presentation based on your answers.

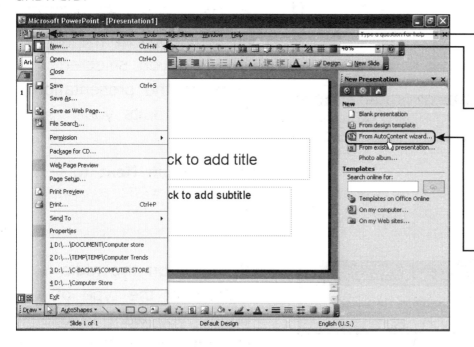

1. Click on **File** in the menu bar. The File menu will appear.

2. Click on **New**.

*The **New Presentation task pane** appears at the right-hand side of the screen.*

3. Click on **From AutoContent Wizard** to create a new presentation using the AutoContent Wizard.

*The **AutoContent Wizard** window appears.*

This area describes the wizard.

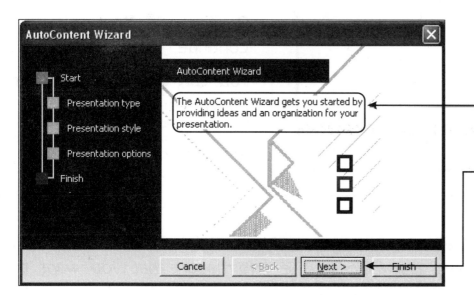

4. Click on **Next** to start creating your presentation.

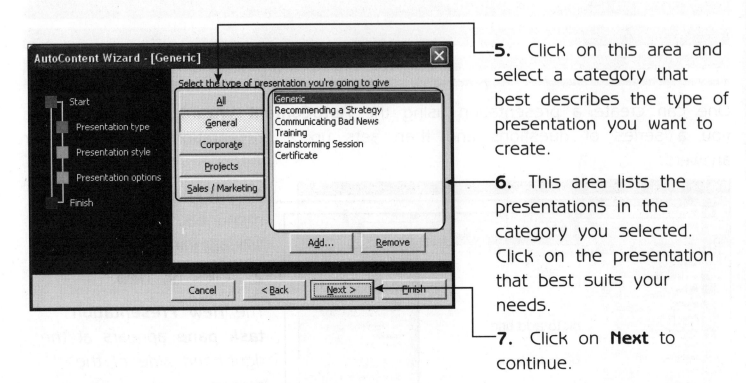

5. Click on this area and select a category that best describes the type of presentation you want to create.

6. This area lists the presentations in the category you selected. Click on the presentation that best suits your needs.

7. Click on **Next** to continue.

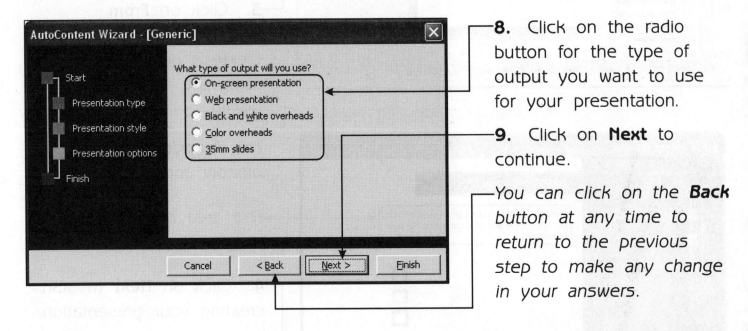

8. Click on the radio button for the type of output you want to use for your presentation.

9. Click on **Next** to continue.

*You can click on the **Back** button at any time to return to the previous step to make any change in your answers.*

❖ *The AutoContent Wizard allows you to specify a title for the first slide in your presentation. You can also specify the information that you want to include in each slide.*

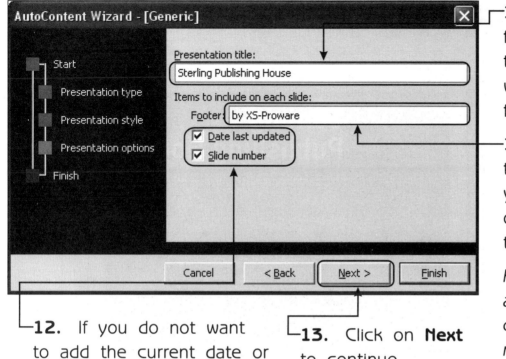

10. Type in the title for the presentation in this area, which you want to include on the first slide.

11. To add a footer text to each slide in your presentation, click on this area and then type the text.

PowerPoint will automatically add the current date and slide number to each slide in your presentation.

12. If you do not want to add the current date or slide number, click the checkmark off from the option you do not want to add.

13. Click on **Next** to continue.

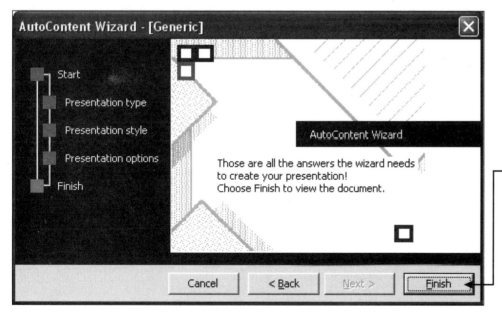

The wizard indicates that you have provided all the answers needed to create your presentation.

14. Click on **Finish** to create your presentation.

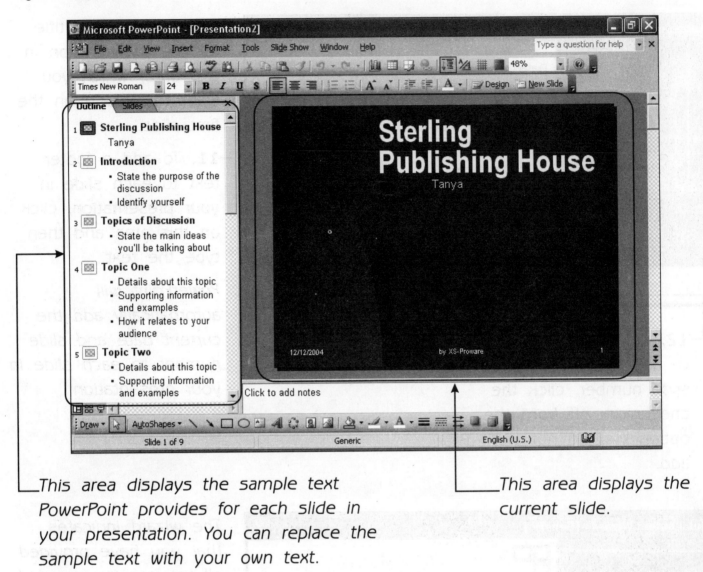

This area displays the sample text PowerPoint provides for each slide in your presentation. You can replace the sample text with your own text.

This area displays the current slide.

3. Creating a Blank Presentation

Creating a Blank Presentation with Design Template

Design and color can be added to a presentation with the help of **Design Template**. The color scheme, font, font size and layout of a presentation is determined by the template. By using the **Slide Design - Design Template** task pane, you can select a particular design template.

For example, if you are interested in changing the template for this presentation from the Default Design to Capsules, perform the following steps to apply the Capsules design template:

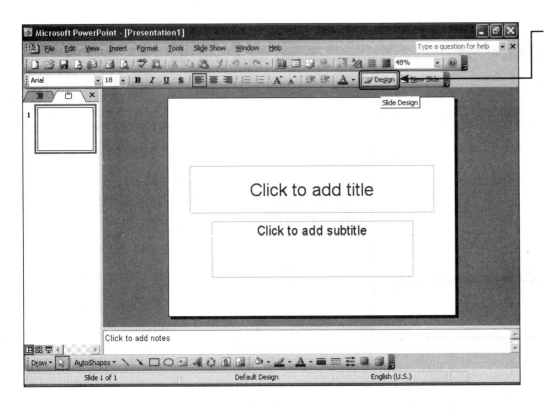

1. Click on the **Slide Design** button on the Formatting toolbar.

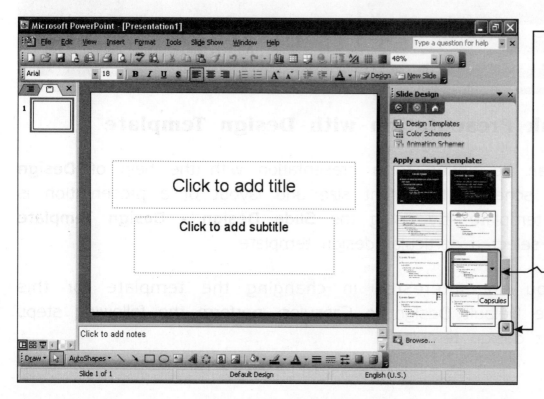

2. Click on the down scroll arrow to scroll through the list of design templates until Capsules is displayed in the **Available For Use** area.

3. Click on the **Capsules** template.

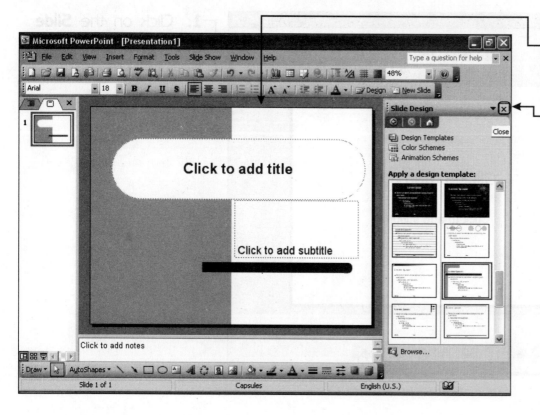

The template is applied to Slide 1.

*When the template has been applied to the Slide, click on the **Close** button in the **Slide Design** task pane to close the pane.*

Creating the Title Slide

With the exception of a blank slide, PowerPoint assumes that every new slide has a title. To make 'creating a presentation' easier, any text typed after a new slide display becomes the title text in the title text placeholder. The presentation title is **Computer Guide**. Perform the following steps to create the title slide for this presentation:

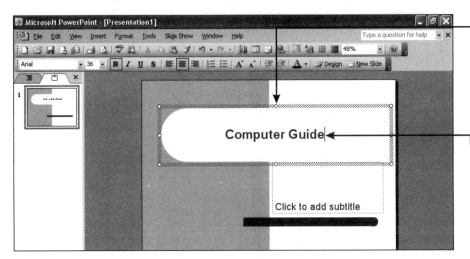

1. Click on the title text placeholder box, which is labeled, '**Click to add title**'.

2. In the title text placeholder, type **Computer Guide** and do not press the ENTER key.

*The title text, **Computer Guide**, gets displayed in one line in the title text placeholder and in the Slides tab. The insertion point is displayed after the letter '**e**' in **Guide**.*

Entering Text in Subtitle

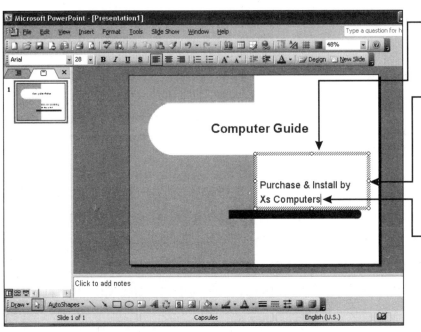

1. Click on the subtitle text placeholder box, which is labeled, '**Click to add subtitle**'.

2. In the subtitle text placeholder, type your text, like **Purchase & Install by,** and then press the **ENTER** key to move to the next line. Type **Xs Computers** but do not press the **ENTER** key.

*The subtitle text gets displayed in the subtitle text placeholder and the Slides tab. The insertion point is displayed after the letter '**s**' in **Computers**.*

Adding a New Slide by Slide Layout

After creating the title slide, your following step is to make the next slide. Normally, whenever a presentation is being created, in addition to slides, one can add text, graphics or charts as well. Whenever a new slide is added, PowerPoint uses the Title and Text Slide Layout.

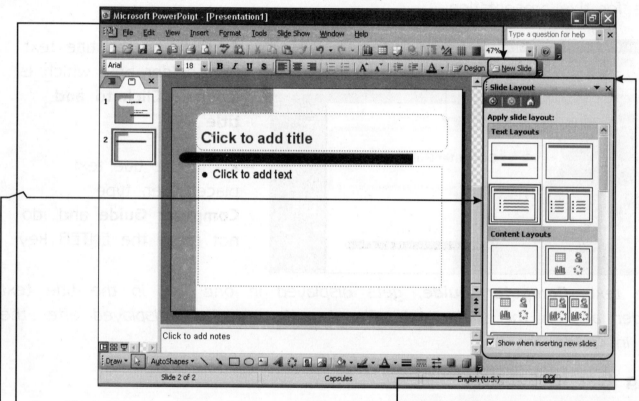

1. Click on the **New Slide** button on the Formatting toolbar.

*The **Slide Layout** task pane appears for you to choose the layout of slide. After the Title and Text slide layout has been selected, slide 2 of 2 gets displayed on the status bar.*

2. After choosing the layout of the slide from the Slide Layout task pane, click on the **Close** button on the Slide Layout task pane to close it.

A layout for a slide can be changed at any time during the creation of a presentation by clicking on **Format** on the menu bar and then clicking on **Slide Layout**. You can also click on **View** on the menu bar and then click on **Task Pane**. You can then double-click on the slide layout of your choice from the Slide Layout task pane.

Using Outline Tab

The **Outline** tab provides a quick and easy way of creating a presentation. **Outlining** allows you to organize your thoughts in a structured format. It is basically a summary of thoughts, presented as headings and subheadings. When a presentation is created, it is often used as a preliminary draft.

The slide text gets displayed along with a slide number and a slide icon in the tabs pane. Body text is indented below the title text and objects such as pictures, graph, or tables do not get displayed. When a slide does not contain objects, the slide icon is blank. Except for color and paragraph style, the attributes for the text on the Outline tab are the same as in Normal view.

When you start a new presentation, PowerPoint initially displays it in Normal View. To type the outline, click on the **Outline tab** in the tabs pane. Perform the following steps to display the Outlining toolbar:

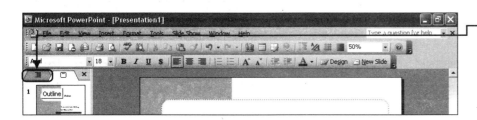

1. Click on the **Outline tab**, which is located in the tabs pane.

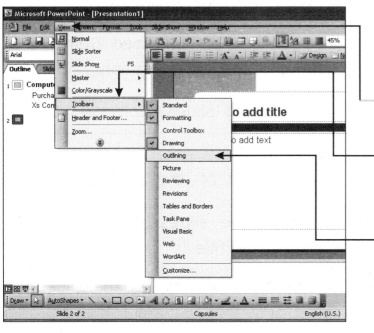

The tabs pane increases and the slide pane decreases in size, when the Outline tab is selected.

2. Click on **View** on the menu bar. The View menu will appear.

3. Place your mouse pointer on the **Toolbars** in the View menu. The Toolbars submenu will appear.

4. Click on **Outlining** on the Toolbar's submenu.

The Outlining toolbar gets displayed.

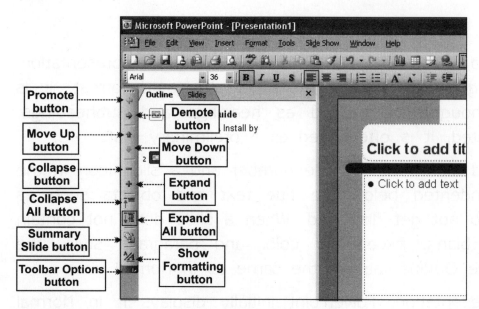

You can create and edit your presentation with the Outline tab. The outline tab makes it easy to sequence slides and to relocate the title text and body text from one slide to another.

Buttons on the Outlining Toolbar

Promote: Moves the selected paragraph to the next-higher heading level (up one level, to the left).

Demote: Moves the selected paragraph to the next-lower heading level (down one level, to the right).

Move Up: Moves the selected paragraph and its collapsed (temporarily hidden) subordinate text above the preceding displayed paragraph.

Move Down: Moves the selected paragraph and its collapsed (temporarily hidden) subordinate text below the following displayed paragraph.

Collapse: Hides all but the title of the selected slides. Collapsed text is represented by a grey line.

Expand: Displays the titles and all collapsed text of the selected slides.

Collapse All: Displays only the titles of all the slides. Text other than the title is represented by a grey line below the title.

Expand All: Displays the titles and all the body text for all the slides.

Summary Slide: Creates a new slide from the titles of the slides you select in slide sorter or normal view. The summary slide creates a bulleted list from the titles of the selected slides. PowerPoint inserts the summary slide in front of the first selected slide.

 Show Formatting: Shows or hides character formatting (such as bold and italic) in normal view. In the slide sorter view, it switches between showing all text and graphics on each slide and displaying titles only.

Toolbar Options: Allows you to select the particular buttons you want to display on the toolbar.

Creating a Presentation Using Outline Tab

Some of the functions of an Outline tab are to view the title and body text, add and delete slides, drag and drop slide text, drag and drop individual slides, promote and demote text, save a presentation, print an outline, print slides, copy and paste slides or text to and from other presentations, apply a design template and import an outline.

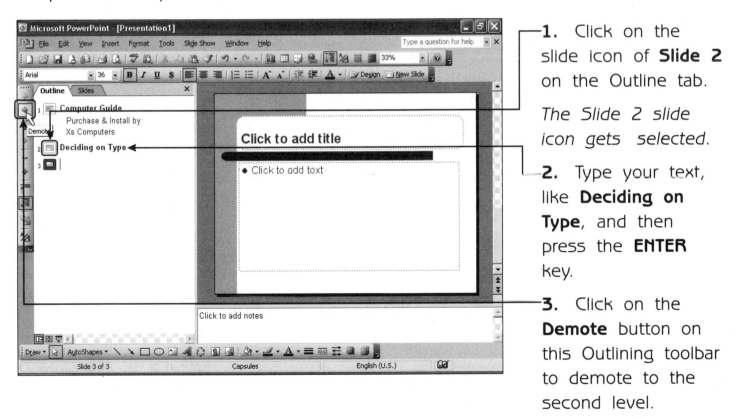

1. Click on the slide icon of **Slide 2** on the Outline tab.

The Slide 2 slide icon gets selected.

2. Type your text, like **Deciding on Type**, and then press the **ENTER** key.

3. Click on the **Demote** button on this Outlining toolbar to demote to the second level.

The title for Slide 2, Deciding on Type, gets displayed and the insertion point is in position to type the first bulleted paragraph. A bullet is displayed to the left of the insertion point.

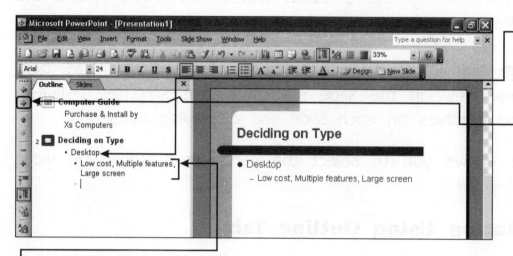

4. Type your text, eg **Desktop**, and then press the **ENTER** key.

5. Click on the **Demote** button to place the insertion point in position to type the second bulleted sub-paragraph.

6. Type your text, eg **Low Cost, Multiple features, Large screen** and then press the **ENTER** key.

Till now Slide 2 displays three levels: the title on the first level; bulleted paragraphs on the second level; and bulleted sub-paragraphs and the insertion point on the third level.

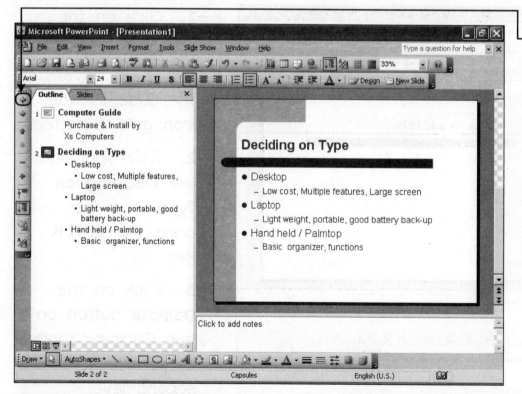

7. Click on the **Promote** button once to bring the insertion point to the second level paragraph.

8. Type in the remaining text in the same way as you did in your earlier steps and press the Enter key in your second slide.

Slide 2 is complete in Outline tab view.

Adding a Slide on the Outline Tab

While creating the first slide in slide **tab** view, when a new slide is added in normal view, PowerPoint defaults to a Text slide layout with a bulleted list. This action occurs on the Outline tab as well. One way to add a new slide on the Outline tab is to promote a paragraph to the first level by clicking on the Promote button on the Outlining toolbar until the insertion point or the paragraph gets displayed at the first level. At this point a slide icon is displayed. To add a slide on the Outline tab, follow the steps given below:

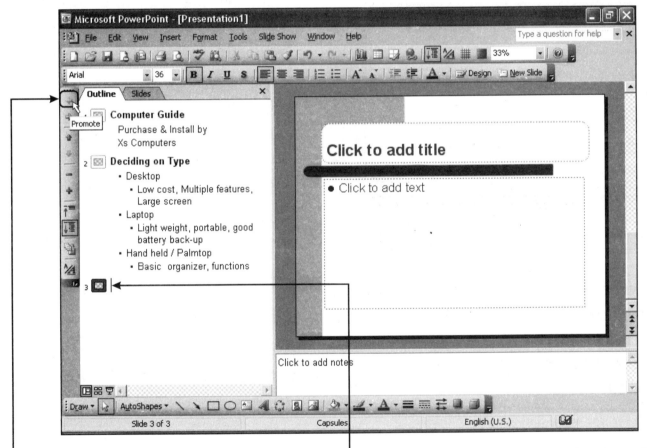

1. Click on the **Promote** button on the Outlining toolbar until the next slide icon gets displayed.

The Slide 3 icon gets displayed indicating that a new slide has been added to the presentation. The insertion point flashes, showing that it is in a position to type the title for Slide 3 at the first level.

4. Saving, Opening and Formatting a Presentation

Saving a Presentation

Once a presentation is created, you can save it for future use. This allows you to review and make changes to the presentation later.

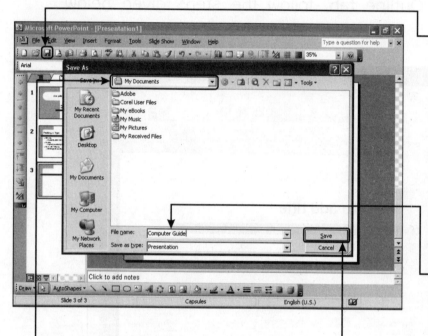

1. Click on the **Save** button (⊞) on the Standard toolbar to save your presentation. The **Save As** dialog box appears.

If you have previously saved your presentation, the Save As dialog box will not appear since you have already named the presentation.

2. Type a name for the presentation in the **File name**:

—*This area shows the location where PowerPoint will store your presentation. You can click on this area to change the location.*

3. Click on the **Save** button to save your presentation.

PowerPoint saves your presentation in hard disk by the name that you have given to it.

Closing a Presentation

1. Once you have finished working on a presentation, click on the **Close** button (**x**) on the top right-hand corner in the title bar to close the presentation. The presentation disappears from your screen.

Opening a Saved Presentation

You can open a saved presentation to view the presentation on your screen and also make changes in it.

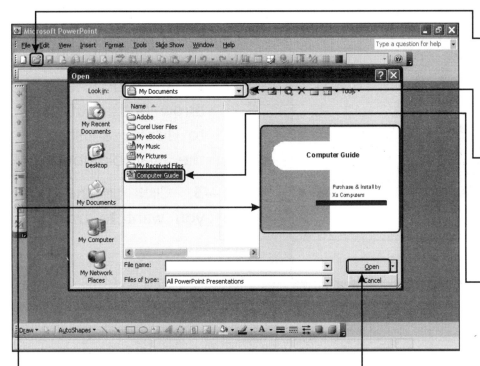

1. Click on the **Open** button in the standard toolbar to open a presentation. *The **Open** dialog box appears.*

This area shows the location of the displayed presentations. You can click on this area to change the location.

2. Click on the name of the presentation you want to open and view.

─*This area displays the first slide in the presentation you selected.*

3. Click on the **Open** button to open the presentation.

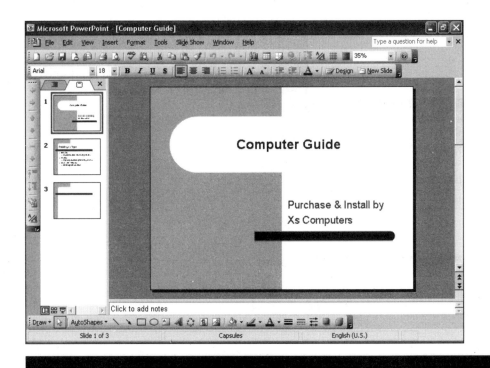

The presentation opens and appears on your screen. You can now review and make changes in the presentation.

*The **Title bar** area displays the name of the open presentation.*

Changing the Font of the Text

You can change the font of the text to enhance the appearance of a slide.

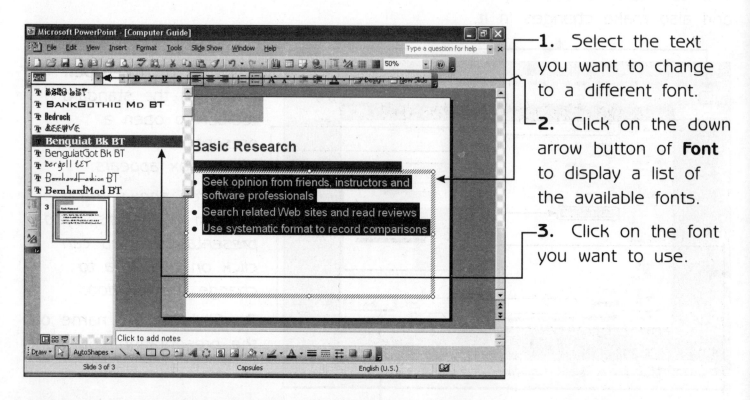

1. Select the text you want to change to a different font.

2. Click on the down arrow button of **Font** to display a list of the available fonts.

3. Click on the font you want to use.

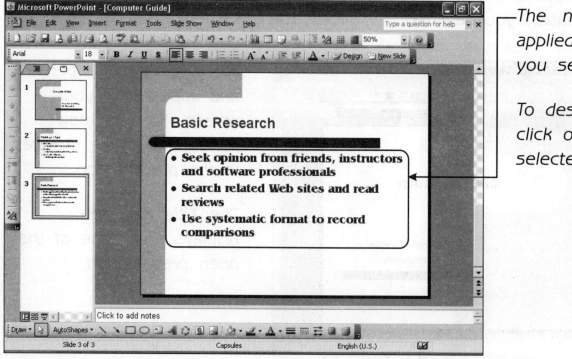

The new font is applied to the text you selected.

To deselect the text, click outside the selected area.

Changing the Size of the Text

You can increase or decrease the size of the text on a slide in PowerPoint.

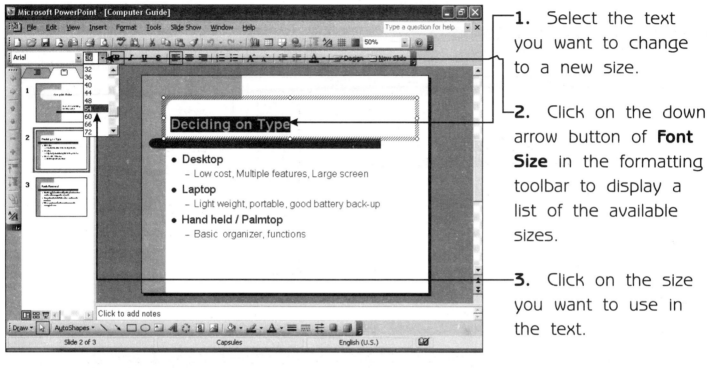

1. Select the text you want to change to a new size.

2. Click on the down arrow button of **Font Size** in the formatting toolbar to display a list of the available sizes.

3. Click on the size you want to use in the text.

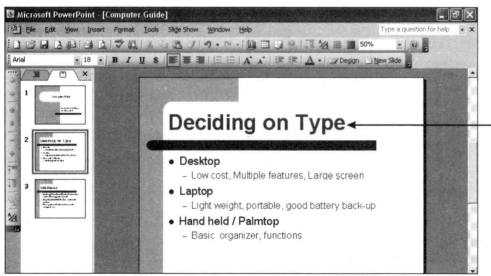

The text you selected changes to the new size.

To deselect the text, click outside the selected area.

To Quickly Change the Size of the Text

1. After selecting the text, click on the **Increase Font Size** button (A) or **Decrease Font Size** button (A) in the formatting toolbar to increase or decrease the size of the text respectively.

Changing the Style of the Text

You can make a text **bold, italicize, underline or add a shadow** to it in order to emphasize information on a slide.

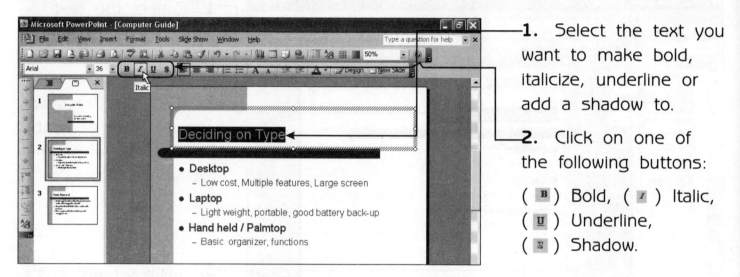

1. Select the text you want to make bold, italicize, underline or add a shadow to.

2. Click on one of the following buttons:

(**B**) Bold, (*I*) Italic,
(**U**) Underline,
(**S**) Shadow.

The text you selected will appear in the new style.

To deselect the text, click outside the selected area.

To remove a bold, italic, underline or shadow style, repeat steps 1 and 2.

Changing the Alignment of the Text

You can change the alignment of the text on a slide to enhance the appearance of the slide.

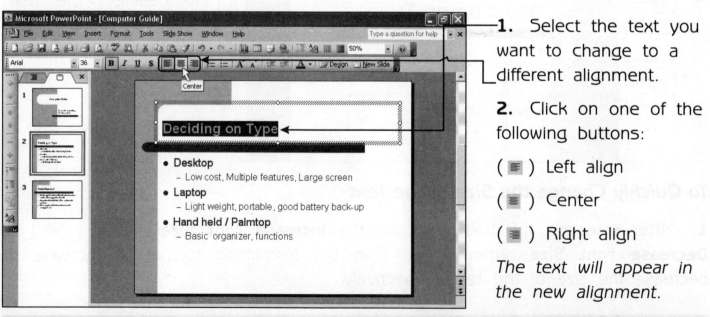

1. Select the text you want to change to a different alignment.

2. Click on one of the following buttons:

(≣) Left align

(≣) Center

(≣) Right align

The text will appear in the new alignment.

Changing the Color Scheme of Slides

You can change the color scheme of all the slides in your presentation.

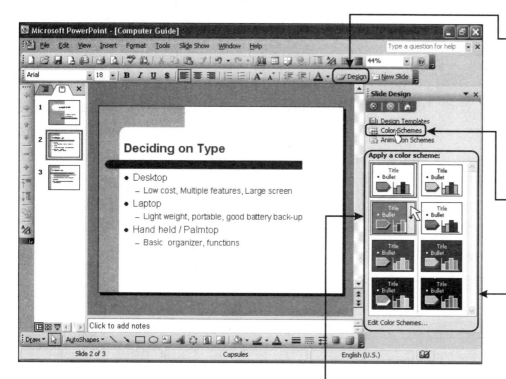

1. Click on the **Slide Design** button on the formatting toolbar.

The Slide Design task pane gets displayed.

2. Click on **Color Schemes** in the Slide Design task pane.

The available color schemes gets displayed in this area.

You can use the scroll bar to browse through the color schemes.

3. Click on the color scheme that you want to use in your presentation.

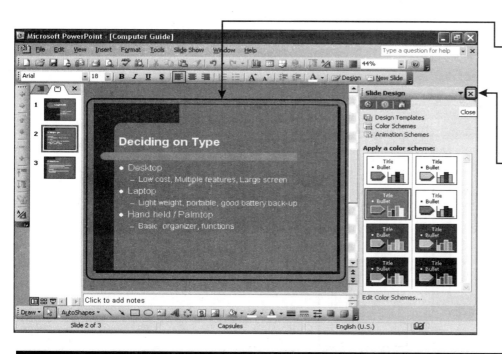

4. The color scheme you have selected will apply to all the slides in your presentation.

5. Click on the **Close** button to close the Slide Design task pane.

Repeat step 3 if you want to change the color scheme of your presentation.

5. Adding Graphics

Changing Slide Layouts

With the help of PowerPoint you created the presentation by applying the Title Slide layout for Slide 1 and the Title and Text layout for the other slides in the presentation. These layouts are the default styles. **Layout** specifies the arrangement of placeholders in a slide. Arranged in various configurations, these placeholders can contain text, such as the slide title or a bulleted list or they can contain contents, such as clips, pictures, charts, tables and shapes. A slide layout determines the placement of the text in relationship to the content. A slide layout can be chosen with the help of a **Slide Layout task pane**. Perform the following steps to change the layout of a slide.

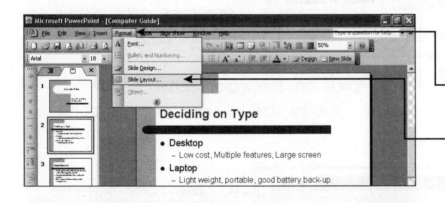

1. Display the slide you want to change to a new layout.

2. Click on **Format** in the menu bar.

3. Click on **Slide Layout**.

The **Slide Layout task pane** appears.

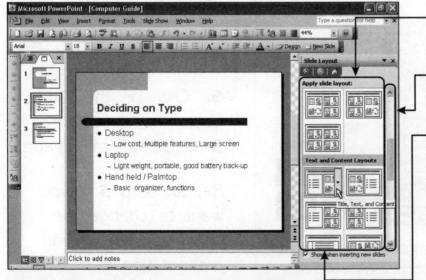

This area displays the available layouts.

You can use the scroll bar to browse through the layouts.

4. Click on the layout you want to use.

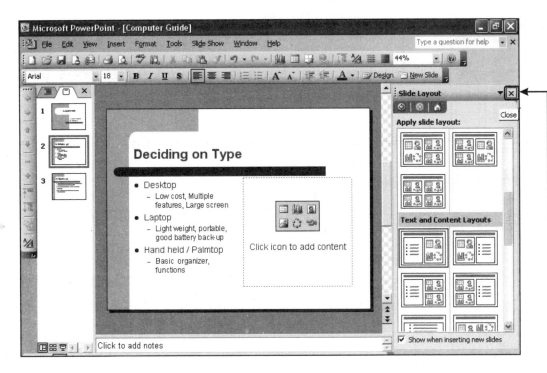

The slide changes to the layout you selected.

*To select a different layout, repeat step **4**.*

5. Once you have selected the slide layout, you can click on [**x**] to close the Slide Layout task pane.

The layout is applied to the Slide. PowerPoint moves the text placeholder containing the bulleted list to the left side of the slide and automatically resizes the text. The content placeholders on the right side of the slide displays the message: **Click icon to add content**.

Adding a Clip Art Image

A **Clip Art** image can be added to a slide to make your presentation more interesting and entertaining.

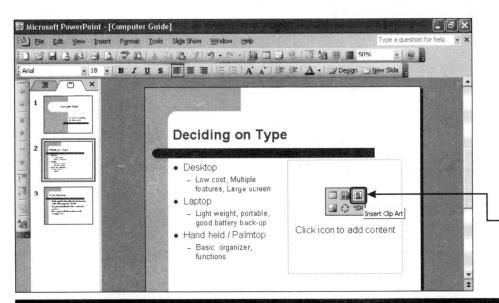

1. Display the slide you want to add a **Clip Art** image to.

2. Change the layout of the slide to one that includes a placeholder for a **Clip Art** image.

3. Click on the **Clip Art** icon (🖼) to add a **Clip Art** image.

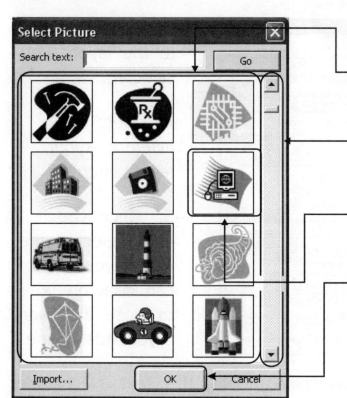

The **Select Picture** dialog box appears.

This area displays the Clip Art images you can add to your slide.

You can use the **scroll bar** to browse through the clip art images.

4. Click on the **Clip Art image** you want to add to your slide.

5. Click on the **OK** button to add the clip art image to your slide.

The Clip Art image appears on the slide.

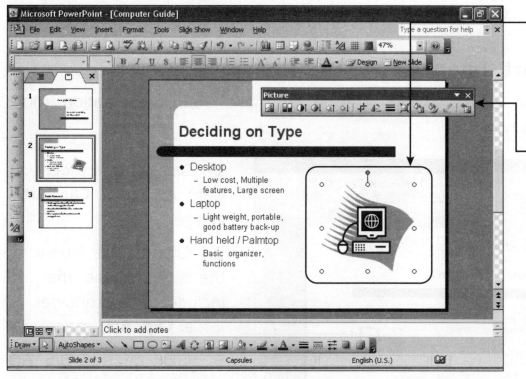

The handles (o) around the clip art image allow you to change the size of the image.

The Picture toolbar also appears, displaying buttons that allow you to make changes to the Clip Art image.

To deselect a Clip Art image, click outside the image.

To delete the Clip Art image, just click on the clip art image you want to delete and then press the **Delete** key on the keyboard.

6. Viewing and Printing Slide Show

Using Slide Sorter View

The **Slide Sorter View** allows you to look at several slides at one time, which is why it is the best way to evaluate a presentation for content, organization and overall appearance.

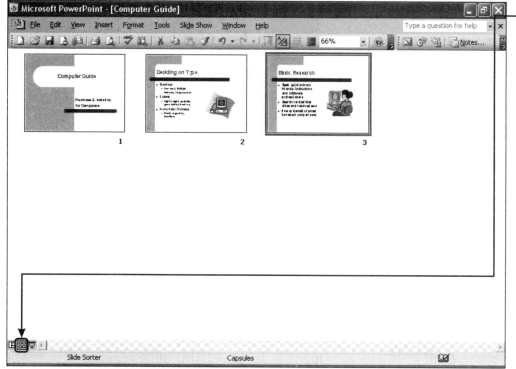

1. Click on the **Slide Sorter View** button at the lower left side of the PowerPoint window.

*PowerPoint displays the presentation in the **Slide Sorter View**. Slide 1 is selected because it was the current slide on the Outline tab.*

The Slide Sorter View button is selected.

With the help of the Slide Sorter view, you can change the order of the slides in your presentation. This is useful when you want to reorganize the ideas in your presentation.

You can also remove a slide you no longer need from your presentation. This is useful if a slide contains incorrect or outdated information.

Viewing a Slide Show

You can view a slide show of your presentation on your computer screen. A slide show displays one slide at a time using the entire screen.

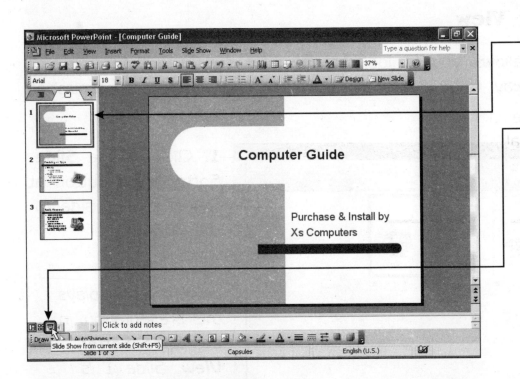

1. Click on the first slide you want to view in the slide show.

2. Click on the Slide Show icon (🖳) to start the slide show.

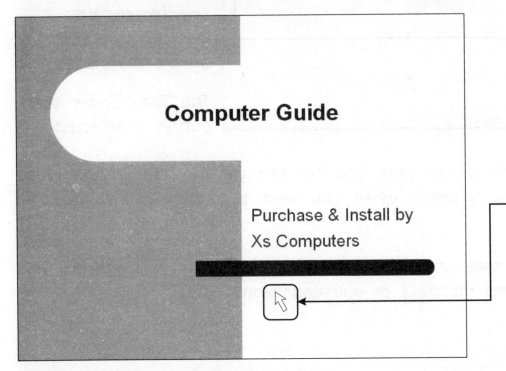

The slide you selected appears on your screen.

*You can press the **Esc** key to end the slide show at any time.*

3. To display the next slide, click anywhere on the current slide.

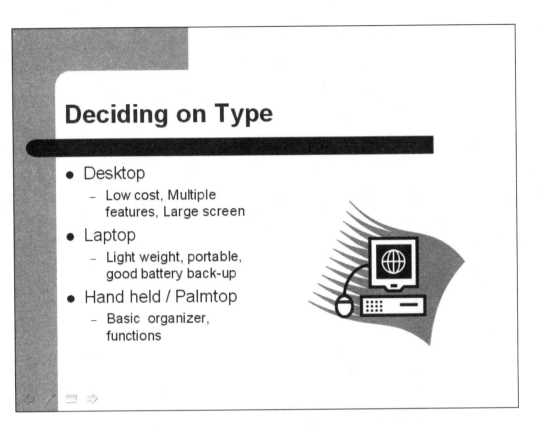

The next slide appears.

To return to the previous slide, press the **Backspace** *key on the keyboard.*

End of slide show, click to exit.

4. Repeat step **3** until this screen appears, indicating that you have reached the end of the slide show.

5. Click on the screen to exit the slide show.

Previewing a Presentation before Printing

The Print Preview feature is used to see how your presentation will look when printed. This confirms that the presentation is printed the way you want.

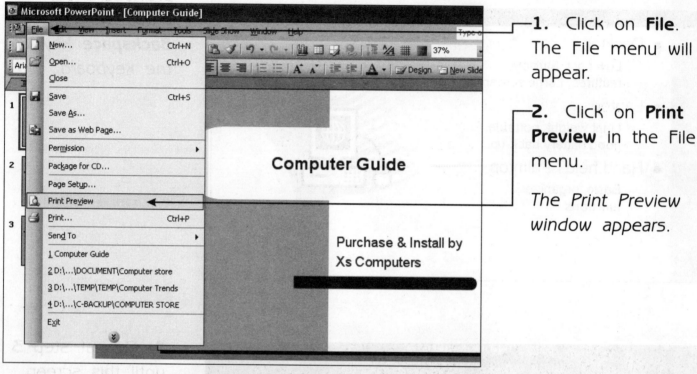

1. Click on **File**. The File menu will appear.

2. Click on **Print Preview** in the File menu.

The Print Preview window appears.

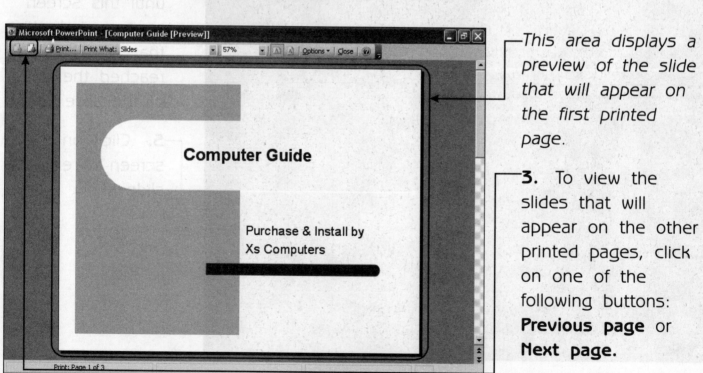

This area displays a preview of the slide that will appear on the first printed page.

3. To view the slides that will appear on the other printed pages, click on one of the following buttons: **Previous page** or **Next page.**

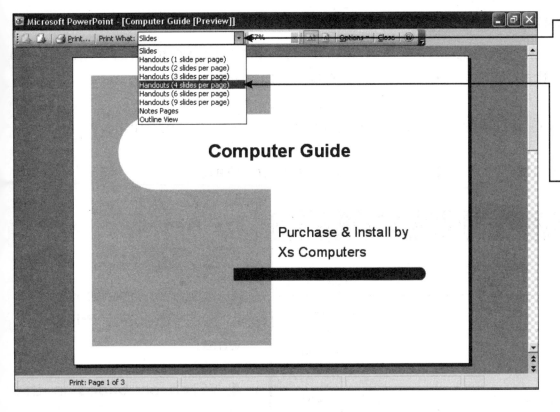

4. To preview all the slides of your presentation before printing, click on this area.

5. Click on number of slides of the presentation you want to preview.

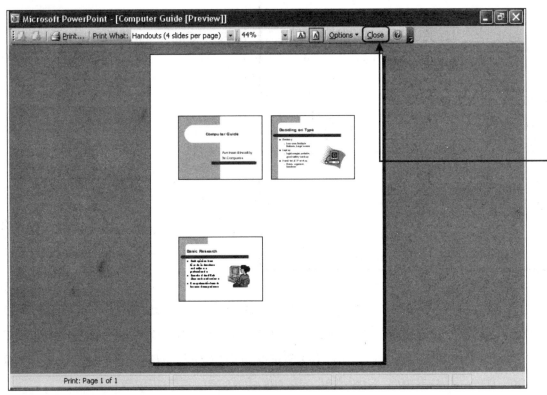

A preview of the slides of the presentation you selected appears on your screen.

5. When you finish previewing your document, click on the **Close** button to close the Print Preview window.

Printing Presentation Slides

You can also get a paper copy of each individual slide of your presentation. To get the printout of the slides, perform the following steps:

1. Check the printer according to the printer's manufacturer instructions.

2. Click on **File** on the menu bar and then click on **Print**.

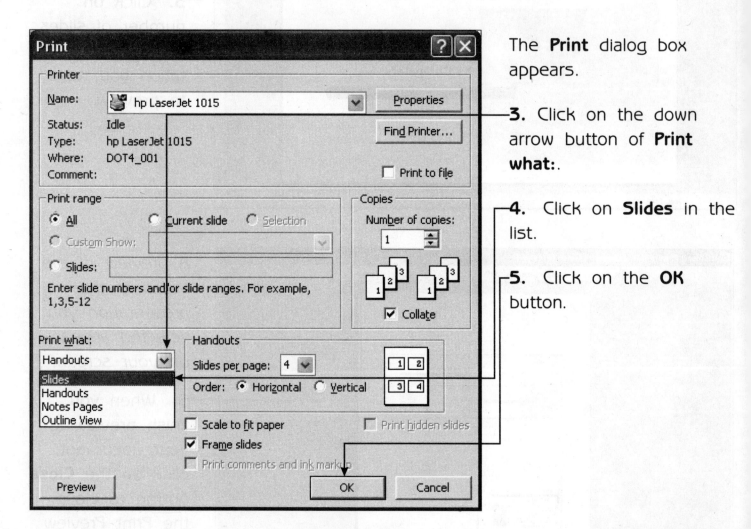

The **Print** dialog box appears.

3. Click on the down arrow button of **Print what:**.

4. Click on **Slides** in the list.

5. Click on the **OK** button.

*The **printer icon** in the tray status area on the Windows taskbar indicates a print job is processing. After several moments, the presentation begins printing on the printer. When the presentation has finished printing, the printer icon in the tray status area on the Windows taskbar is no longer displayed.*